South African Labour Issues

By Mitta Xinindlu

About the Book

This is the research the author undertook in 2017, studying and gaining labour statistics and irregularities in South Africa. Hopefully, the situation will change post the nomination of the new president, Cyril Ramaphosa.

About the Author

Talented and a versatile writer, also a labour analyst with over five years in the labour industry. Successfully generated labour related articles, reports, proposals, and informed reviews. An enthusiastic and creative individual, adept at quality work and enthusiastic about analysing leadership and management types - doing so with tremendous integrity and common sense.

The goals of this project are to explore the current labour assumptions in South Africa, especially in relation to race and governmental management and/or leadership. Thus, also finding the causes of, and solutions to, the current labour problems affecting Black graduates. It is also important for the government of South Africa to analyse this report and gain relevant information about the issues at hand that need to be corrected through intelligent decision-making processes.

Having worked in different labour sectors, including financial, manufacturing, engineering and academic, there has been a realisation of, among other possible issues, a trend that is displayed through irregular hiring processes. With this first-hand experience, it's an important goal to voice out the root cause for high employment in South Africa through this project and raise awareness.

Hopefully, the South African government will take this into consideration and take the issue as an urgent problem.

Foreword

This book explores and reports the identified labour issues and possible remedies. This is a channel from which South African citizens, particularly government key individuals, can seek facts and relevant opinions for the purposes of planning and execution. The short-term goals include raising awareness for the upcoming 2019 national elections, providing live information and social media statistics. Additionally, in the long-term, this platform will be relevant for future research and advancement planning in creating job opportunities, particularly, for Black graduates. It will also act as a benchmark in the future, when assessing whether there have been any changes regarding the South African labour market.

Audience

This website has been made publicly available to grant access to the South African government. The navigation through the website is made simple to not frustrate the audience. The audience is encouraged to click on the links, pictures, and texts where the mouse allows when hovering. However, since it is a public domain, many parties are also encouraged to draw statistical data from this project for their own research purposes. Therefore, anyone with an interest and who finds the information embedded on this website useful should feel free to engage and contact the author for further discussions. Moreover, the audience should be confident that the information on here is well-researched, credible and relevant.

Context

The content on this website has been or will be included in articles written and released by the author to the public in the form of single pieces. The information will be further explained in labour related interviews should there be a need. The information on this website is based on current analyses and the audience should be aware that statistics can and may change as and when the circumstances in the labour market change.

The multi-media items included in this research have been obtained from the internet, unless stated otherwise.

South African Labour Issues

The Cause for High Unemployment in South Africa

South Africa is economically identified as a developing country due to insufficient resources that could be readily available for the empowerment of its citizens. As a developing country, South Africa still faces many challenges, including a high rate of unemployment. Consequently, the majority of those who are unemployed, or who are deprived of the opportunity to be employed, are Black graduates. Many Black South Africans have blamed apartheid for this irregular economic flaw, and on the other hand, many White South Africans have blamed the government's mismanagement tactics. South Africa is a diverse country that has a history of apartheid where Black people were ill-treated and deprived of economic opportunities. One of the tactics of the apartheid leaders used was to deprive the Black race of quality education; thus, leaving them in unfair economic state. It must be noted that apartheid also introduced □Bantu education□, which did not allow many Black people to access university education. The reader must note that it was only in 1994 that many Black people regained easy access to quality education.

The ANC political party, which has a majority of Black people as members, has been running the country since 1994 when South Africa regained its democracy. Thus, it has been 23 years since the official dispensation of apartheid; meaning that the ANC government has had 23 years to rectify the unfairness that resulted from apartheid. Moreover, they have had the same number of years to distribute resources, which include employment opportunities, especially to those who were previously disadvantaged.

Considering the Blacks versus Whites' assumptions, this project aims to explore the root cause for the high unemployment rate among Black graduates in South Africa.

Central Research Question (CRQ)

What is the root cause for the high unemployment rate among Black graduates in South Africa?

☐Project's exigency☐ (an urgent need or demand)

The introduction of social media has exposed an urgent need for employment opportunities, particularly for the Black race. Over the recent years, many Black graduates have been posting their graduation pictures and unemployment situations to beg for jobs through social media. Through their stories, they have implied that both the private and public sectors do not give Black graduates job opportunities. Twitter, for example, has been the leading platform on which Black graduates beg for employment opportunities. Prior to the social media excessive usage, the masses depended on statistics released by either the government or private research companies; thus, not allowing the public to closely scrutinise the unemployment rate of graduates. However, this free access to live, valid and reliable statistics has also raised a debate and a blame game within the two racial groups — Blacks and Whites.

Currently, there has not been anyone who has publicly taken responsibility or accountability for the increasing unemployment rate that Black graduates face, hence the blame game, and the lack of a properly defined root cause. According to Kaoru Ishikawa's fishbone diagram claims that one must define various factors that could be the cause before commencing with a development plan.

Black people in this research are mainly Africans and do not include Coloureds, Indians or Chinese.

Project's Kairos (right opportune moment)

South Africans will be voting for a new government and/or president in the year 2019. Subsequently, the findings and relevance of this project will be informative and influential to the voting process. It is at this time that the plans to improve the situation must be taken with urgency; therefore, also indicating a need to obtain informed and researched analyses. The year 2017 marks a critical point for the current government because, in the previous year, the ANC lost a significant percentage of voters in the provincial elections. Thus, highlighting the possibility of the same results coming up again in the 2019 national and presidential elections.

This project, by exploring and finding the root cause for the unemployment imbalance in South Africa, has a potential to indicate that many voters, which are the youth* may negatively affect the poll results. Having a job in South Africa is viewed as an achievement; Black South Africans study and obtain degrees because of the belief that education will enable them to find employment. Therefore, if the youth are unsatisfied due to lack of employment or opportunities, the voting results may also be affected.

Talking to the Right Audience

This project is addressed to the South African governmental bodies because they are the decision makers when it comes to labour issues in the country. They have the power to ensure that Black graduates are considered; they can also change the existing labour rules, challenge placed policies, or introduce new ways that labour processes can be handled in this country. It is a known fact that governmental influence is effective in changing the lifestyles and situations of countries. Additionally, the governmental bodies have the power to rule and overturn obsolete processes, which no longer serve the purpose of the nation. Therefore, to have an informed readership who can make a difference is vital, especially for the Black unemployed graduates in South Africa. The current government can incorporate the ideas and findings stated in this project into their strategy planning, and the prospective leaders can use this project as a source for both their campaigns and the planning process.

Additionally, the race blame for the failure of the system may be lessened.

The South African Labour Stakeholders

Stakeholders are defined as members, either legal entities or humans, who have an interest in the outcome of an organisation, a group or a project. The stakeholders to this project are all citizens of South Africa, particularly, the Black graduates. South Africans are all affected, directly or indirectly, by the lack of opportunities. This project is important because in raising an awareness by exploring the root cause for the high unemployment among Black graduates, all stakeholders will be able to plan effectively, address the issues at hand, and continue to explore proper processes that can be used to rectify labour imbalances in

South Africa.

Sources & Methods

This research requires that I consider both qualitative and quantitative approaches. Targeted sources for this project will be (i) the internet: Online academic journals, news outlets, and including social media platforms. The internet provides immediate and easily accessible information; (ii) purchased magazines because they provide approved and timely public information; and (iii) governmental or political members through interviews because they tend to have relevant and first-hand information that may not be readily available to the public.

The Labour Stakeholders

Stakeholder 1: Hendrik van Broekhuizen

MLA Work Cited
Van Broekhuizen, H. "Graduate unemployment and Higher Education Institutions in South Africa." Stellenbosch Working Paper Series: WP08 (2016). Print.

Background
This is an article that was submitted by Hendrik as a Working Paper, in which he summarises his PHD research progress regarding labour relations in South Africa.

Credibility
According to Econ.3x3.org, Hendrik van Broekhuizen is pursuing his PhD studies at the Stellenbosch University while he is also an employee of the Research on Socio-Economics Policy (ReSEP) group. He has had a vast experience in the field of labour analysis and has been involved in various projects with the aim to analyse labour markets, poverty, inequality, and education. He is currently

focusing on establishing a link between university education and unemployment. In his past projects, he has focused in applied micro econometrics, behavioural economics, labour economics, and the economics of education. Therefore, he is qualified, knowledgeable and equipped with experience.

Purpose
Hendrik states that universities at which graduates attend have a major influence in whether they obtain employment post-graduation. In his research project, he addresses the inequalities of the South African labour market by collecting data through multiple surveys. In addition, he proves that employment is not just one of the major problems in South Africa, but it is also racially aligned.

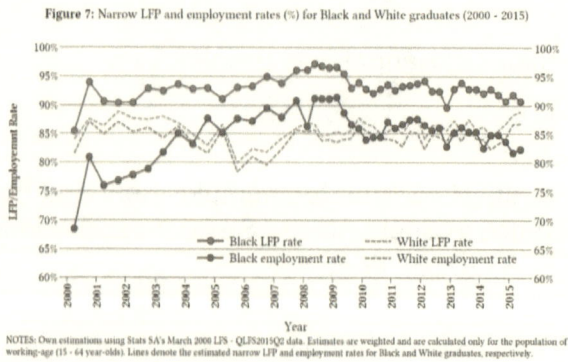

Figure 7: Narrow LFP and employment rates (%) for Black and White graduates (2000 - 2015)

NOTES: Own estimations using Stats SA's March 2000 LFS - QLFS2015Q2 data. Estimates are weighted and are calculated only for the population of working-age (15 - 64 year-olds). Lines denote the estimated narrow LFP and employment rates for Black and White graduates, respectively.

Situation of the Source
As a labour market researcher, Hendrik is interested to prove that there is an existing imbalance within the market. He further states that the imbalance places the economy at a disadvantaged position. In one of his sections, he criticises the existing literature regarding the issue, in which he shows that not much research has been done.

In his presentation, one can observe that from the years 2000 to 2015, Black graduates have been leading the unemployment

16

field. In addition, the rate of Black unemployed graduates is constantly increasing; it was at approximately 15% in 2015 and rose to above 16% in 2016.

Strategies
He uses quantitative data to draw the attention of his audience. Furthermore, in his literature, he follows a probabilistic cell-matching approach and combines it with multiple computational counting and common time-invariant group-specific variables. Appealing to Logos in this type of research is plausible because his audience are the scholarly calibre.

Interaction with other annotations: Hendrik and Mbuyiseni
Both Henrik's journal article and the manifesto as presented by Mbuyiseni agree that South Africa is facing a high unemployment problem. Delivered in the form of documents, and available over the internet, both articles are concerned that the current government are not as active as they ought to be. Lastly, both articles indicate that the rate of unemployment has increased over the years, instead of decreasing as initially promised by the current governing party, the ANC. The writers are both young and educated, pursuing PHD studies; nevertheless, they have different background in terms of politics and governance. Hendrick is an observer, whereas Mbuyiseni is a member of the decision makers in the parliament. Although their influence is different in comparison, their roles are important.

Evaluation of the Source
He concludes that the universities from which Black graduates obtain their education are the influence on the high employment rate. His conclusion does not seem to be convincing because, in his claims, he states that even though Black graduates attend the same universities as Whites and obtain the same qualifications, the result still implies that Blacks are still not skilled enough to be employable. Moreover, although he has presented the facts

through his collected data, he is still of the view that although this is a problem, it is not something that requires immediate action.

How will Hendrik's article be used?
Hendrik's article is important for the South African labour field, simply because it introduced a link that, although it has flaws, can still be used to dig deeper into the problem, and in establishing more solutions.

Stakeholder 2: Max du Preez

MLA Work Cited
Du Preez, M. "Who is to blame for South Africa's failure." Opinions Columnists. News 24, 14 June 2016. Web. 23 March 2017. <*http://www.news24.com/Columnists/MaxduPreez/who-is-to-blame-for-south-africas-failures-20160614*>.

Background
This is an article that is published through one of the leading newspaper/media houses in South Africa. Max subjectively criticises political leaders and politics as they happen in current time.

Credibility
Max du Preez is a South African columnist, journalist, author and documentary filmmaker. As a journalist prior 1994, he worked to expose the unfairness of apartheid and its injustices. He played a huge role in the South African transformation and established Vyre Weekblad, a newspaper that had a goal of exposing apartheid.
Max du Preez was also involved in the South African Truth and Reconciliation Commission process; he produced content with which he promoted unity. He continues to be a relevant and important figure in the media and has won several awards,

including the Courageous Journalism and the Yale Globalist International Journalist.

Purpose

In his article, Max is concerned with the current economic state of South Africa. He aims to raise awareness regarding the inaction of the ANC party and how it affects many people, mainly, young Black people.

Situation of the Source

This article is of an opinion of a well-known author in South Africa, an author who is very influential in terms of the economy, and whose arguments have been included in many publications. Max has further substantiated this article with many more and similar arguments. His approach is fearless, and he aims to challenge those whose mind-sets have not set yet.

Strategies

Max's article is based on both facts and emotions. He uses his journalistic presentation approach and draws the interest of his audience by using current and valuable information.

Interaction with other annotations: The Constitution and Max du Preez

In The Constitution, all the plans for the development of South Africa and the protection of the citizens were established by the Legal parties with the influence of the democracy which the ANC fought for and won in 1994. Accordingly, Max du Preez, in his article, questions the morality of the country in terms of the promises made by the ANC government post 1994. Moreover, he challenges the Whites who, in his opinion, refuse to acknowledge the damage that the apartheid caused. Max is a member of the public and he benefits from The Constitution in terms of his Rights being protected.

Evaluation of the Source

He states that the ANC has failed to build a new and better nation. According to Max, the ANC party has had an advantageous position since 1994, from which they obtained legal control. However, with all that control, the ANC has failed to offer better education system, especially for young Black people.

How will the article be used?

Max's article is interesting because he approaches the situation with less bias. He challenges both sides of the history and both racial groups equally. Due to the credibility of his work, this article will be used as an influential piece to the research in terms of referencing and learning the history of South Africa and its freedom, or lack thereof, regarding the unemployment rate among Black graduates.

Stakeholder 3: Mbuyiseni Ndlozi

MLA Cited Work

Ndlozi, M.Q. 2014. "Here is the EFF Manifesto, each page is critical...let us spread it to all corners of South Africa for victory on 7 May, 2014." Facebook, 1 March 2014. Web. 30 March 2017. <https://www.facebook.com/mbuyiseni/posts/10152268973774066>.

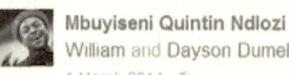

Mbuyiseni Quintin Ndlozi added 7 new photos — with Mokhitli William and Dayson Dumela.
1 March 2014

Here is the EFF Manifesto, each page is critical... let us spread it to all corners of South Africa for victory on 7 May, 2014

Background

Mbuyiseni, as the Spokesperson of the Economic Freedom Fighters in South Africa, delivered the party's Manifesto via the social network Facebook, which addressed many issues in South

Africa. In Section A of the EFF's Manifesto, he reminded their audience that there are still many irregularities in South Africa, especially, regarding poverty and unemployment.

He stated that the time to rescue South Africa from deep levels of inequality, poverty, starvation, unemployment and under-employment had finally arrived.

Credibility
Mbuyiseni is the Spokesperson of the Economic Freedom Fighters (EFF), in which he is the youngest. He has obtained his education from the University of Witwatersrand where he is also pursuing a PhD in Political Sociology. He has reported to be forced into politics when his uncle was wrongfully arrested by the apartheid government in 1992. Currently, as a Member of Parliament, he aims to ensure that all Rights are protected and that the interests of the citizens of the Republic are equally respected.

Purpose
Mbuyiseni and his party, through the Manifesto, aimed to remind South Africans, Blacks, that the promised economic equality by the ANC in their 1994 elections' manifesto had not been met. Thus, Mbuyiseni highlighted that Blacks were and are still disadvantaged and deprived of economic privileges; they are deprived of employment opportunities.

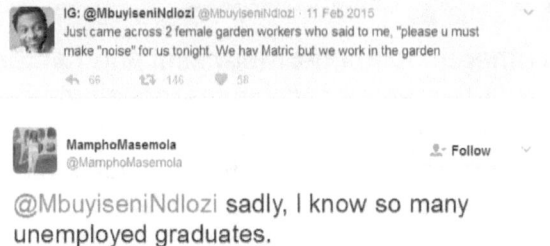

@MbuyiseniNdlozi sadly, I know so many unemployed graduates.

Situation of the Source

The manifesto has been a key discussion point among EFF followers, as a result, the EFF have shaken the state of politics in South Africa with a more forceful and revolutionary manner, which is quite new to the South African politics. Moreover, it has been easy for people to believe in what Mbuyiseni has to say. For example, he has been given the nickname "People's Bae" due to both his looks and overall intelligence in his approach. Mbuyiseni has repeatedly proven his commitment in bettering the lives of African Black graduates; he has actively challenged the educational system and the President's views in parliament. Black graduates can relate to him and have found him influential because he is an educated Black young man, who has a positive vision for his fellow people.

Strategies

Mbuyiseni is a political figure; therefore, his agenda is political – particularly, with the view to enhance the lives of Black people in South Africa. This is a common strategy with which many Black politicians approach the audience. The manifesto was used to lobby votes from people. However, even though the lobbying was successful, he has continued to attempt to live up to the Manifesto, which with his team, he delivered to all South Africans. Mbuyiseni appeals mostly to people's emotions rather than ethics. His party in general uphold emotions more than morality, which is a flaw. Importantly, Mbuyiseni also presents statistics, however, which are mostly highlighted to criticise the ANC government and not to necessarily present concrete solutions.

Interaction with other annotations: Mbuyiseni and Twitter

Both Mbuyiseni and Twitter, as my sources, speak to one another. Twitter has been one of the platforms in which Mbuyiseni communicates his values, visions and those of his party. Many graduates and/or youth have sent him pleas via Twitter, requesting him to change the state of the high unemployment rate in South Africa. Although Twitter is a risky source, it must be acknowledged as relevant because South Africa, like some other technologically influenced countries, uses Twitter as a platform to an open discussion between politicians and the citizens of the Republic.

kingfardin
@Thekgomos
🔾 Follow ∨

@ZolaNdwandwe @MbuyiseniNdlozi so is the rest of 8000 graduates who are unemployed. have been told the same story by their white professors

Nozipho
@Knowzy_
🔾 Follow ∨

Dear @MbuyiseniNdlozi . Can you please tell Parliament to prioritize creating permanent jobs for graduates? Internships aren't enough.

Ramahlale
@kuliwachina
🔾 Follow ∨

@lutiii123 @Julius_S_Malema @MbuyiseniNdlozi how many black graduates are begging for jobs on street corners. Racist exclusion#malema

Song
@Song56556106
🔾 Follow ∨

@MbuyiseniNdlozi fighter hw do we as EFF help graduates

thami
@mpetshentt

@MbuyiseniNdlozi. Plz start by transforming the mining industry as it is the most racist. Even graduates r subjected to racism by uneducate

rachel
@lakhlakh6

@MbuyiseniNdlozi If the graduates dont get jobs,they wont be able tp pay NIFSAS BACK.So instead of playing these dumb tricks, get busy.

sandile
@sand_inmotion

@MbuyiseniNdlozi: how can you help kzn unemployed Social worker students graduates?, Mec Weziwe threatened 2blacklist them when they marched

Michelle Munyai
@michelliciousm

@MbuyiseniNdlozi can you please address the issue of unemployed social work graduates who were recipients of the #DSD scholarships

zeepour
@zipogwsdha1

@GardeeGodrich @MbuyiseniNdlozi @Julius_S_Malema @EFFSouthAfrica @FloydShivambu .Justice for these Graduates

Mathlavani Matsheke
@sukumeta

@Julius_S_Malema @effjoburg @EFFSouthAfrica @AdvDali_Mpofu @MbuyiseniNdlozi under Eff job must wait for graduates

Evaluation of the Source

Mbuyiseni is a valid, influential and reliable source. As a member of parliament, his opinion carries a heavy weight in terms of decision-making or economic evaluation. His strategies are also relevant as he involves the public and updates them accordingly. The release of the manifesto via Facebook was a strategical move, which gained them more audience and/or public favour.

How will Mbuyiseni's article/Manifesto be used?

The manifesto will be used to show that opposition parties and their members are as equally concerned with the lack of employment for Black graduates. In addition, I have sent Mbuyiseni a questionnaire in which I asked that he elaborate on his views as stipulated in the Manifesto and those of the EFF party regarding the high unemployment rate among Black graduates in South Africa. The reason for the request for clarity is that this topic was not specified in detail in the manifesto; therefore, it would be valuable to have more information. Mbuyiseni's response had not been received when this report went for publication.

The Constitution of the Republic of South Africa

MLA Work Cited

The Constitution of the Republic of South Africa. The Bill of Rights. RSA. 11 October 1996. Web. 28 March 2017.

Background

The Constitution is divided into different sections and from those sections this research will analyse the following:

1. Section 9: The Right to equality

2. Section 10: The Right to Human Dignity

3. Section 23: Labour relations

Credibility

The Constitution of the Republic is the main legislation that governs the Republic.

Purpose

The Constitution of the Republic was created:

to— Heal the divisions of the past and establish a society based on democratic values social justice and fundamental human rights; Lay the foundations for a democratic and open society in which government is based on the will of the people and every citizen is equally protected by law; Improve the quality of life of all citizens and free the potential of each person; and Build a united and democratic South Africa able to take its rightful place as a sovereign state in the family of nations." - The constitution of the Republic of South Africa.

The quoted text explains the purpose of The Constitution, which its relevance to this research is from a compliance perspective. This research analyses the current South African situation and its governance by assessing whether The Constitution is being followed as per the quote.

Situation of the Source

The Constitution is the overpowering legislation which governs and directs the country. In the legislation, the rights of the citizens are established and clearly defined. Since this is the main legal document in South Africa, the details of labour specifics are also included. This research particularly analyses three Sections from the Constitution, which prove to hold much relevance as they state that all citizens have: (i) a Right to Equality, including employment opportunities; (ii) a Right to Human Dignity, [see case; Dendy v University of the Witwatersrand and Others (2015/03/2005) ZAGPHC]; and (iii) a Right to Fair Labour Practices, which emphasises that all potential employees, regardless of race, are equal, eligible and fit to work, unless proven otherwise.

Strategies

The Constitution, as a legal document, is presented in such a way that all the citizens of the Republic would be equally protected, provided for, prioritised, and elevated. This document seeks to appeal to ethics, morality and justice. Therefore, also ensuring that its purpose is achieved in the eyes of the Law and of the people of South Africa.

Interaction with other annotations: The Constitution and Max du Preez

In The Constitution, all the plans for the development of South Africa and the protection of its citizens were established by Legal parties with the influence of the justice system and the democracy which the ANC fought for and won in 1994. In accordance, Max du Preez, in his article, questioned the morality of the country in terms of the promises made by the ANC government post 1994. Moreover, he challenged the Whites who, in his opinion, refused to acknowledge the damage that the apartheid caused.

Evaluation of the Source

The Constitution of South Africa details all the Rights to which the citizens are entitled. It is credible, current, and a legal reference for courts, ordinary people, and governmental bodies.

How will the Constitution be used?

The Constitution will be used for referencing, aligning current views with those of others, and as a tool in challenging the current labour system.

Stakeholder 4: Twitter Community

MLA Work Cited

Various Selected Twitter Users. Twitter.com. n.p. 11-24 March 2017. Web. 24 March 2017.

Background

Van Zyly reported in 2015 that the South African youth are active on Twitter; their number is included in the 2.68 million Users as of year 2015. Accordingly, the referenced Users have been selected based on their relevance to this research.

Credibility

Canini, Suh and Pirolli reported in their research that Twitter is a social media tool that is also used as a platform from which its Users can communicate, share ideas, microblog, and send messages. The content is actively updated approximately every split second on Users' timelines, depending on whom they choose to follow.

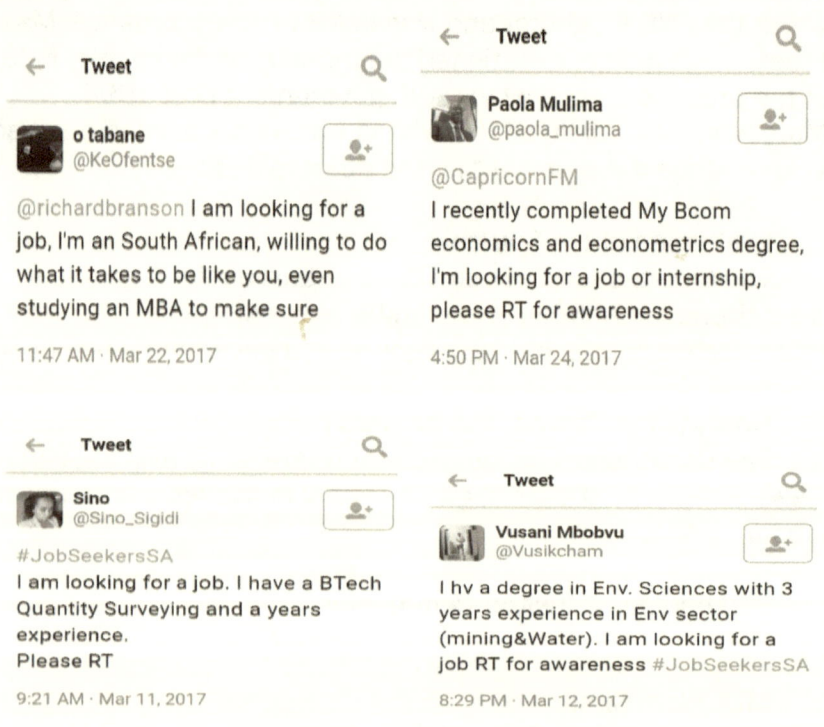

← Tweet 🔍

o tabane
@KeOfentse

@richardbranson I am looking for a job, I'm an South African, willing to do what it takes to be like you, even studying an MBA to make sure

11:47 AM · Mar 22, 2017

← Tweet 🔍

Paola Mulima
@paola_mulima

@CapricornFM

I recently completed My Bcom economics and econometrics degree, I'm looking for a job or internship, please RT for awareness

4:50 PM · Mar 24, 2017

← Tweet 🔍

Sino
@Sino_Sigidi

#JobSeekersSA
I am looking for a job. I have a BTech Quantity Surveying and a years experience.
Please RT

9:21 AM · Mar 11, 2017

← Tweet 🔍

Vusani Mbobvu
@Vusikcham

I hv a degree in Env. Sciences with 3 years experience in Env sector (mining&Water). I am looking for a job RT for awareness #JobSeekersSA

8:29 PM · Mar 12, 2017

Purpose

As a social platform, Twitter provides immediate information, which this research will use. Twitter, also as a source, aims to provide credible or valuable data, although it might be limited in nature. The data regarding Black university graduates obtained from Twitter is essential as it indicates a small possible sample of unemployed Black graduates who are in desperate need for employment.

Situation of the Source
The selected tweets indicate that there are graduates who are desperate for jobs even though they have gotten the minimum requirement for one to obtain a professional job in South Africa, which is a quality education. The data was extracted from Twitter and the people who posted the cited Tweets have not been contacted to solidify their claims.

Strategies
There is over 90% interaction between South African corporations and the public according to MG.co.za; this indicates that businesses in the Republic prioritise Twitter as one of the platforms from which they reach the public. Likewise, Twitter has become a platform on which Black South African graduates, among other activities, beg for jobs. They do this with the hope that a potential employer might respond to their outcry. Some graduates use facts in proving their capabilities while some appeal to the emotions of those who run corporations, or those who have a potential to make a difference in their lives.

Interaction with other annotations
Twitter is freely accessible to anyone; as a result, people such as Mbuyiseni interact with the public through this platform. Notably, Twitter is undeniably relevant to the South African communication field.

Evaluation of the Source

Twitter is not entirely reliable on its own and must be used with caution. Any information that is posted on Twitter is public domain, therefore, it's legitimacy may be questionable to a certain extent. Thus, for this research, Twitter will be used as an informational tool. However, it must be noted that its relevance and importance to this research remains high and unquestionable because had it not been for Twitter, this research would not have been pursued.

How will Twitter be used?
This research will use Twitter to estimate the total sample of those who are Black, graduates and are unemployed in South Africa.

Stakeholder 6: ANC 1994 Manifesto Audience

MLA Work Cited
ANC. "1994 National Election Manifesto". 1994. Web. 16 April 2017. <http://www.anc.org.za/content/1994-national-elections-manifesto>.

Background
The manifesto of the ANC is a document that the ANC presented to the people in 1994, in the hope that what it presented would convince the people to vote for the ANC and put them in power. Consequently, with this document, the ANC managed to lobby voters and to achieve their goal, which was to govern the Republic.

Credibility
This is an official document which was submitted to the courts of law and the general members of the Republic.

Purpose

The manifesto was delivered with the purpose of convincing South African voters that the ANC political party can challenge the unfair structures that the apartheid government had built in South Africa. In this manifesto, the ANC promised to improve the lives of all South Africans, especially of those who were disadvantaged and abused by the apartheid system and its believers.

Situation of the Source
This manifesto was released in 1994, right after the Republic regained its freedom from the apartheid government. Therefore, the content was heavily situated on the events that had occurred prior 1994; consequently, promising improvements in housing schemes, education, employment, unity, equality, openness, improved quality of life, and many other things which seemed lucrative to those who had been deprived of the treatment that is good and suitable for all human beings.

Strategies
The ANC used the apartheid circumstances to convince or manipulate the minds of those whom they targeted. The ANC's manifesto appealed to the pathos of the people in 1994. This manifesto appealed to the emotions and the feelings of the people. In addition, the ANC presented the manifesto in a way that indicated its purpose as moral, legal, and ethical, therefore, also appealing to ethos.

Interaction with other annotations: the ANC Manifesto and The Constitution
The manifesto of the ANC was built on the promises of the Constitution of the Republic. Consistently, the manifesto mentioned the Bill of Rights, which is a critical section in The Constitution and which this research will examine in part. In mentioning the Bill of Rights, the ANC manifesto promised to uphold and enforce the legislation accordingly. The documents are both legal representatives of the public. Accepted and recognised

by the justice system, they uphold promises on which the country is governed.

Evaluation of the Source
The ANC manifesto is a well-presented document and it carries a heavy weight in contributing to the democratic history of the Republic, especially when considering its content and the state of the audience during the time it was presented. Currently, in 2017, the manifesto of the ANC seems to contrast with the current actions of the ANC government in South Africa. Many of the statements that were presented in 1994 through this manifesto have become questionable.

How will the manifesto be used?
Notably, the ANC is the current governing party in South Africa. They have been in power since this manifesto was released in 1994. Therefore, every word that they had presented in the manifesto is important to this research as each word will or may be used to analyse the current state of the country and the success, if any, that the party achieved regarding the provision of jobs to the people of the Republic, and Black graduates included. Finally, the manifesto will be used to assess how the ANC government failed to live up to some of the promises that they made through this manifesto. In conclusion, the manifesto is a critical source in forming a concrete analysis, recommendation, channel for solutions, and calling the ANC government to action.

My Findings

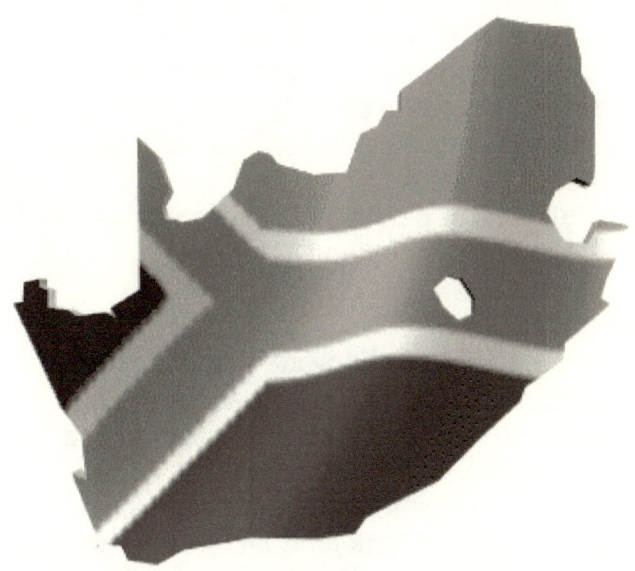

South Africa is economically identified as a developing country due to insufficient resources that are readily available for the empowerment of its citizens. South Africa is a diverse country and has a history of apartheid where Black people were ill-treated and deprived of economic opportunities. Consequently, this has led to lack of enriching opportunities for Black graduates. It is reported that many Blacks blame apartheid for this irregular economic flaw while on the other hand, many Whites blame the government's mismanagement tactics.

The ANC political party, which has many Black members, has been running the country since the 1994 democracy; however, after 23 years, they have not resolved unemployment.

Considering the Blacks versus Whites' assumptions, this project's controlling purpose is to explore the root cause for the high unemployment rate among Black graduates in South Africa. Thus, with the research question: what is the root cause for the high unemployment rate among Black graduates in South Africa?

Finding the root cause to any problem is vital for the development of any efficient plan as according to 1968 Kaoru Ishikawa's fishbone diagram. The purpose also calls upon the ANC government to act and decrease the high unemployment rate among Black graduates, which statistics have proven to be increasing on a quarterly basis.

Black graduates and/or people in this research are Africans and do not include Coloureds, Indians or Chinese.

Project's Exigency

Currently, there has not been anyone who has publicly taken responsibility or accountability for the increasing unemployment rate among Black graduates, hence the blame game and the lack of a properly defined root cause. Fortunately, the introduction of social media has exposed the urgent need for employment opportunities, particularly for Black graduates. Over the recent years, many Black graduates have been posting their unemployment situations to beg for jobs via social media, also implying that both the private and public sectors do not give Black university graduates job opportunities. Twitter, for example, has been the leading platform on which Black graduates beg for employment. Prior to the social media excessive usage, the masses depended on statistics released by either the government or private research companies; thus, not allowing the public to closely scrutinise the unemployment rate of Black graduates.

Stakeholders

In 1999, Sharp, Finkelstein, and Galal defined Stakeholders as members, either legal entities or humans, who have an interest in the outcome of an organisation, a group or a project*. The stakeholders to this project are Black graduates, however, without the exclusion of all the citizens.

Sources & Methods

34

This research considered both qualitative and quantitative approaches. All multimedia content, such as pictures, have been downloaded from the internet.

Project's Kairos
South Africans will be voting for a new government in the year 2019. Consequently, the findings from this project are relevant because they can be informative and influential to the voting process. Regarding the topic, and according to Cohen and Moodley's 2012 research, having a job in South Africa is viewed as an achievement; Black South Africans study to obtain degrees and subsequently which should enable them to find employment. Therefore, if the youth are unsatisfied due to unemployment, the voting results may also be affected.

Audience
This project is addressed to the South African governmental bodies because they have the power to ensure that Black graduates are considered within the labour market; they can also change the existing labour rules, challenge placed policies, or introduce new ways that labour processes can be handled.

Literature Review

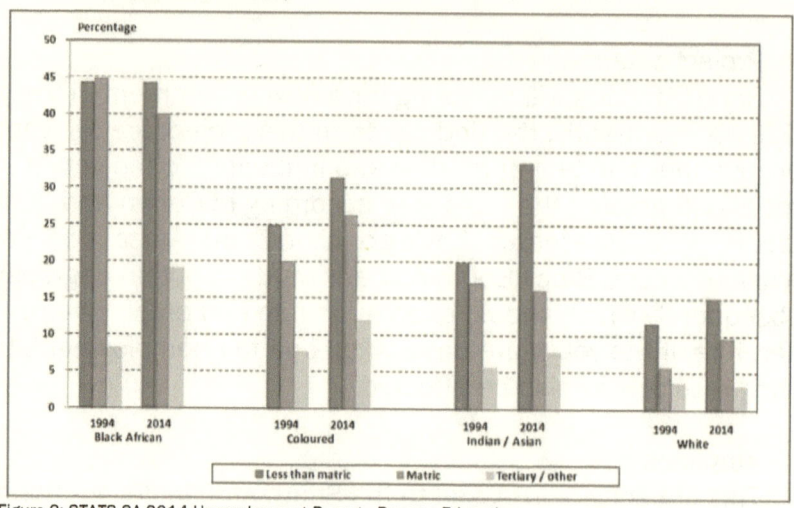

Unemployment* rates by population group and educational level (*based on the expanded definition)

Figure 2: STATS SA 2014 Unemployment Report - Race vs Education

STATS SA, which is the official governmental stats hub releases statistics reports on a quarterly basis. As per figures 1-3, the unemployment rate since 1994 has increased vastly. In 2014, for example, the rate of unemployed Black youth was 40%, and in Quarter 4 of the 2015-year period, the unemployment rate of graduates had contributed to the 49.1% of the unemployed Black youth in South Africa. This also proves that Black people are becoming more alienated from obtaining job opportunities; in only a year, the rate had increased from 40% to 49.1%. Unemployment in South Africa is racially aligned and in confirmation to the STATS report, Hendrik van Broekhuizen reported in 2016 that between the years 2014 and 2015, the rate of unemployed Blacks increased steadily. For example, there were 3 677 561 unemployed Black women between the ages of 15 and 34, who form part of the 49.1%. Fiendishly, almost half of the population in this group who are unemployed in the Republic are reported to be Black women.

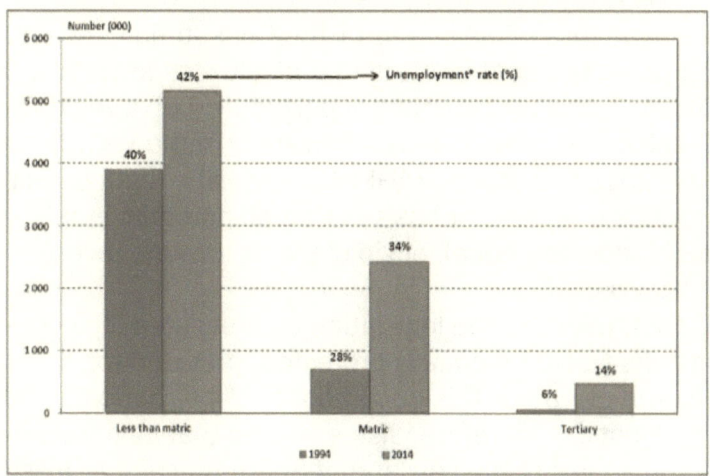

Figure 3: STATS SA 2014 Unemployment Report - Education

Does the above reflect fairness, equality, and the prioritisation of the needs of the Black race in the Republic of South Africa as per The Constitution?

The Constitution of the Republic of South Africa

The Constitution, which governs and oversees the Republic under the promises of providing equality and fairness in terms of economic advancements and improved quality of life seems to be failing the Black race. It must be noted that The Constitution details the Rights to which the citizens are entitled. This legislation is credible, current, and a legal reference for courts, ordinary people and governmental bodies. The Constitution is divided into different sections and from those sections, this research analysed the following:

1. Section 9: The Right to equality

2. Section 10: The Right to Human Dignity

3. Section 23: Labour relations

Since this is the legislation, the details of labour specifics are also critical. The three Sections from The Constitution prove to hold much relevance as they state that all citizens have: (i) a Right to Equality, including employment opportunities; (ii) a Right to Human Dignity, [see case; Dendy v University of the Witwatersrand and Others (2015/03/2005) ZAGPHC]; and (iii) a Right to Fair Labour Practices, which emphasises that all potential employees, regardless of race, are equal, eligible and fit to work, unless proven otherwise.

The Constitution, as the legislation, is presented in such a way that all citizens would be equally protected, provided for, prioritised, and elevated. This document seeks to appeal to ethics, morality and justice. Therefore, also ensuring that its purpose is achieved in the eyes of the Law and of South Africans as also promised in the ANC's 1994 manifesto.

The ANC's 1994 Manifesto

The manifesto of the ANC was presented in 1994 to convince people to vote for the ANC and put them in power. Subsequently, with this document, the ANC managed to lobby voters and to achieve their goal, which was to govern the Republic. The content was heavily situated on the apartheid events that had occurred prior 1994; consequently, promising improvements in education, employment, equality, openness, improved quality of life, and many other things which seemed lucrative to those who had been deprived of the treatment that is good and suitable for all human beings.

Have all the promises been achieved?

The role of Twitter in exposing unemployment

According to Fin24.com, the South African youth are active on Twitter; their number is included in the 2.68 million Users as of the year 2015

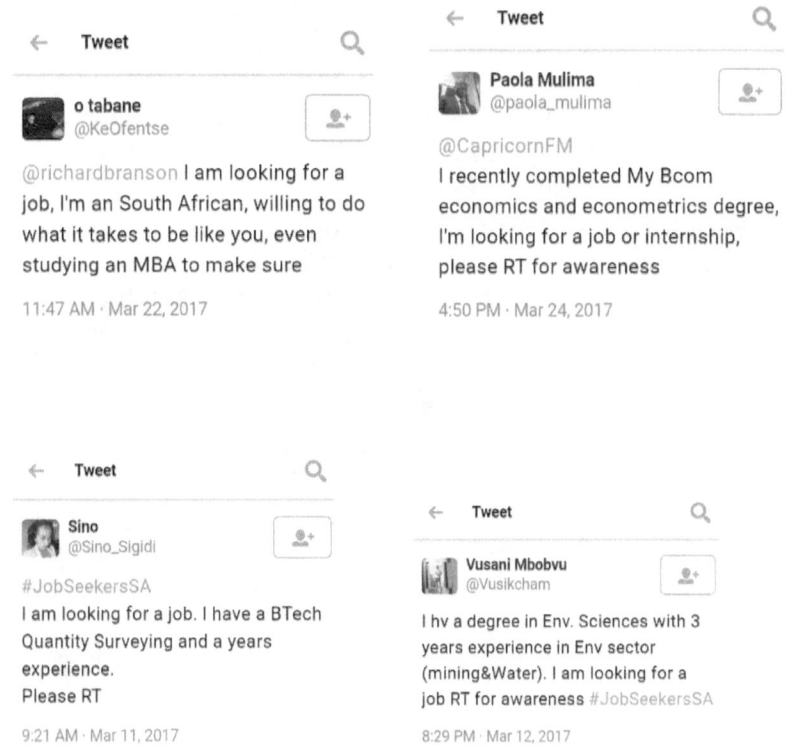

Tweet

o tabane
@KeOfentse

@richardbranson I am looking for a job, I'm an South African, willing to do what it takes to be like you, even studying an MBA to make sure

11:47 AM · Mar 22, 2017

Tweet

Paola Mulima
@paola_mulima

@CapricornFM
I recently completed My Bcom economics and econometrics degree, I'm looking for a job or internship, please RT for awareness

4:50 PM · Mar 24, 2017

Tweet

Sino
@Sino_Sigidi

#JobSeekersSA
I am looking for a job. I have a BTech Quantity Surveying and a years experience.
Please RT

9:21 AM · Mar 11, 2017

Tweet

Vusani Mbobvu
@Vusikcham

I hv a degree in Env. Sciences with 3 years experience in Env sector (mining&Water). I am looking for a job RT for awareness #JobSeekersSA

8:29 PM · Mar 12, 2017

As a social platform, confirmed by van Zyl in 2015, Twitter provides immediate information, which this research considered. Twitter, also as a source, aims to provide valuable data, although it might be limited in nature. The data regarding Black graduates obtained from Twitter is essential as it indicates a small possible sample of many unemployed Black graduates, even though they have obtained the minimum job requirement, which is a quality education.

The views of labour parties

In his research project to address the inequalities of the Republic's labour market, Van Broekhuizen claims that universities at which graduates attend have a major influence in whether they obtain employment post-graduation. Additionally, he states that there exists a racial imbalance within the market, which is economically threatening. In his presentation, one can observe that from the years 2000 to 2015, Black graduates have been leading the unemployment field. Thus, the rate of unemployed Black graduates is constantly increasing; it was at approximately 15% in 2015 and rose to above 16% in 2016.

Labour analysts such as du Preez have criticised the ANC party for their failures. The ANC, as the leading party, who have had 23 years to make a difference to the lives of Blacks have failed to live up to their promises.

EFF is one of the vocal and active parties in the Republic, who are concerned about the failures of the ANC in meeting their promises as per the 1994 manifesto regarding the improvement of the economic status for Black people. In delivering their 2014 manifesto, in Section A, Mbuyiseni Ndlozi, who is the national spokesperson of the party, reminded their audience that there are still many irregularities in South Africa, especially, regarding poverty and unemployment.

The Needed Discussion

Analysis: identifying the root cause for high unemployment among Black graduates in South Africa

The sources to this research state similar concerns and they agree that there is a crisis of high unemployment among the Black race in South Africa. Although van Bruikhuizen states that the root cause is the quality of education which Black people obtain from the universities of their choice, it is hard to believe his claim because of the following facts:

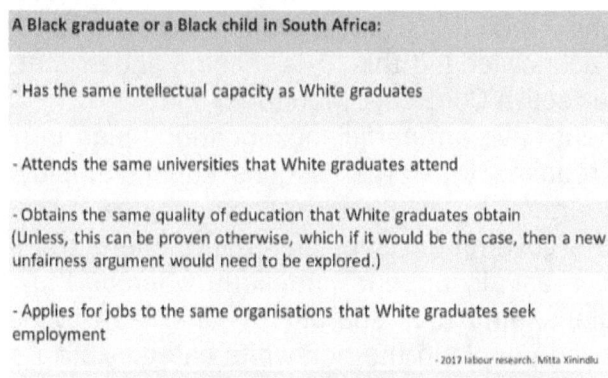

Figure 6: Facts about Black Graduates

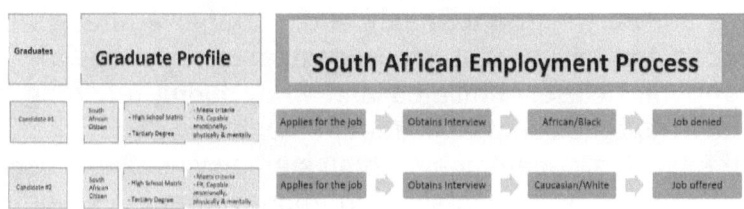

2017. Research. Mitta Xinindlu

Factually, the only reason that Black graduates do not obtain opportunities of employment in the Republic of South Africa is that

41

they are Black. Therefore, the root cause for the high unemployment rate among Black graduates in South Africa is the colour of their skin, that is, being Black.

This raises another discussion: should people's Blackness be the end of them?

Recommendations

The first recommended action is for the ANC political party to acknowledge that they have failed to uphold their promises regarding employment. Psychology studies have proven that the first step to healing is admitting that there is a problem. Once the government has acknowledged this, it is recommended that they must provide an effective Corporate Monitoring Plan.

The government have an inefficient monitoring plan in place, currently, which requires that organisations submit employment statistics on a quarterly basis. Should a company be employing enough Blacks, the government subsidies them. Therefore, many times, the statistics usually appear compliant, whereas they hide the fact that Indians, who are reported by STATS SA to be the majority of employed people in the non-white category are usually included under the 'Black' category since.

The monitoring plan should further be accompanied by effective audits, which are strictly under the government's book; the reason for this is that many companies hire auditors with whom they are closely affiliated and who, during reporting, alter the facts to suit the compliance requirements.

If the Black graduate finally obtains employment, is it because of the companies' will to obtain more money from the government rather than a will to develop a Black child?

Methodology

In performing this research, I followed a multi-source protocol because informing others of factual material requires one to substantiate all claims.

Targeted sources for this project were (i) the internet: Online academic journals, news outlets, and including social media platforms. The internet provides immediate and easily accessible information; (ii) the RSA Constitution, ANC's 1994 Manifesto, and EFF's 2014 Manifesto because they provide contractual material; and (iii) governmental or political members through interviews since they tend to have relevant information that may not be readily available to the public.

The Constitution was used for referencing, aligning current views with those of others, and as a tool in challenging the current labour system. Similarly, the ANC manifesto was used to assess why the ANC government have failed to live up to some of their promises.

The EFF's manifesto was used to show that opposition parties are as equally concerned. Additionally, a questionnaire to Mbuyiseni was sent, in which I asked that he elaborate on his views as stipulated in the Manifesto and those of the EFF party regarding the high unemployment rate among Black graduates.

Other articles and journals were used to draw facts, views and approaches that the ANC government could use in bettering the lives of Black graduates

Limitations

This research does not report on the exact number of unemployed Black graduates who are begging for jobs on Twitter and on the streets. It would, therefore, be valuable for future politically, economically and socially based research to obtain these statistics as they would also encourage the government to act.

Twitter is not entirely reliable on its own and must be used with caution. Likewise, for this research, Twitter was used as an informational tool although its relevance and importance remain high and unquestionable.

Lastly, Mbuyiseni's response had not been received when this report went to publication.

Conclusion

I remember one of the slogans that the ANC party used in 1994; it was powerful and promising, I thought. The slogan was: 'the people shall govern'. With this slogan in mind, Many South Africans and I assumed that this meant our voices, complaints, struggles, and outcries would be heard. Little did we know that the phrase "the people", in this regard, referred only to the ANC elite. The phrase "the people" referred only to those whose concern is for themselves and their families, excluding Black graduates.

Analytically, I stand to believe that there are still those few who remain concerned about the state of the Republic. They should pick up where the 1994 manifesto left off and continue to honour those promises by providing jobs and economic freedom to Black graduates.

The government must remind corporations that being Black does not equal to being stupid, incapable, unskilled, lazy, uneducated, undeserving of employment, and undeserving of a better economic lifestyle. I hereby challenge the government to decrease the 16% unemployment rate among Black graduates to 4% by the year 2019, which is the year for the national election. Should the ANC government be confused as to how to proceed, aligning with The Constitution would be one of the recommendable first steps.

It has been proven that we have the best Constitution in the world. Therefore, each governmental party should ensure that the lives of the citizens are represented as per The Constitution.

The Constitution of the Republic of South Africa is clear in that all economic prospects of everyone, including those of a Black graduate in South Africa, are important and should be protected by all.

www.ingramcontent.com/pod-product-compliance
Lightning Source LLC
Chambersburg PA
CBHW021938170526
45157CB00005B/2345